From Vision to Victory
(How To Triumph Through Praise)

From Vision to Victory
(How To Triumph Through Praise)

by
Bishop Larry D. Trotter

VINCOM, Inc.
Tulsa, Oklahoma

Unless otherwise indicated, all Scripture quotations are taken from *The King James Version* of the Bible.

The Scripture quotation from J. B. Phillips is taken from *The New Testament in Modern English.* Copyright © 1958, 1959, 1960, 1972, Macmillan Publishing Co., New York, New York.

From Vision to Victory
(How To Triumph Through Praise)
ISBN 0-927936-86-0
Copyright © 1995 by
Bishop Larry D. Trotter
Climbing Higher Ministries
944-58 West 103 Street
Chicago, IL 60643
(312) 233-4477

Published by
VINCOM, Inc.
P. O. Box 702400
Tulsa, OK 74170
(918) 254-1276

Printed in the United States of America.
All rights reserved under International Copyright Law. Contents and/or cover may not be reproduced in whole or in part in any form without the express written consent of the Publisher.

Dedication

I am honored to present these "Praise Presentations" to you, my reader.

My dedication goes:

First, to Jesus Christ, my Lord and Savior.

To my loving mother, Dorothy Trotter (Granny), who raised me in the admonition of the Lord.

To my partner in life, my beautiful wife Celeste, and my five wonderful blessings: Laurice, Javon, Brandi, Larry and La Kheem.

To my combined staffs, I salute you for your commitment to the visions God has given, Sweet Holy Spirit Full Gospel Baptist Church Fellowship, the greatest church family in the world.

Special thanks to Brother Jessie Howard, Brother Richard Jackson and Prophet E. Bernard Jordan for your words of prophecy concerning my authorship.

Finally, to my evangelistic ministry, Climbing Higher Ministries.

Contents

Foreword by Biship Paul S. Morton, Sr.
Introduction

1	The Wilderness Days	1
2	Praise — God's Channel of Blessings	13
3	Understanding Praise	19
4	How To Make It Through Your Mess	23
5	What About "Hallelujah"?	29
6	Praise Your Way Through Pressure	35
7	Praise Through Giving	39
8	What Comes After Praise?	43
9	Three-Fold Blessing for Praisers	49
10	How Pure Is Your Praise?	51
11	"I Smell Rain"	57
12	Go On Out Into the Deep!	67

Foreword

The call came through the Word of the Lord, saying, "Make the vision plain." Well, Bishop Larry Trotter has captured the essence of that powerful word in his book entitled, *From Vision to Victory*.

This book will provide you with insight on how to triumph through praise. There are many in ministry who have great gifts, but God has given Bishop Trotter a special anointing as a "prophet of praise." If you desire to be released from the wilderness so that you can receive the benefits of the promised land, you must read this book.

As Christians there are times when we want to praise God only if things are going our way. This book will reveal to you how to praise through the difficult periods in life. The Bible tells us that the "joy of the Lord is our strength." (Nehemiah 8:10.) However, if you allow the devil to steal your strength, the has *you*!

I firmly believe that when you have completed this book, you will recognize the special anointing on this great man of God. He will teach you how to enter into the very presence of God and experience all the wonderful blessings He has for you.

Bishop Paul S. Morton, Sr.
Presiding Bishop
Full Gospel Baptist Church Fellowship

X

Introduction

Praise God! Praise God! Praise God! To praise God is to move from a "wilderness" experience into the victory of your vision. *From Vision to Victory* is the exact place where God desires His great people to be at this hour. God designed us to give praise, to praise with cymbals, harps, voices, timbrels, and stringed instruments. Our purpose in creation is to adore God with praise.

In the unfolding of these formulated pages, I pray that the words will usher in a new order of praise into your life and will answer your questions: How do you get out of the mess you're in? How do you get out of a tough spot? How do you **press toward the mark for the prize of the high calling of God in Christ Jesus** (Philippians 3:14)? How do you break the "pressures" which seem to terrorize your life?

Through the avenue of **praise**, you will tap into all of the blessings of God — His peace, joy, love, wisdom, knowledge, understanding, guidance and all the financial prosperity to do everything He has asked you to do. At the same time, praise from a grateful heart will silence the enemy, abort his plans and expose his traps.

In our society today, we tend to take for granted everything God has already done for us and made available to us. Sometimes we're too selfish to express our gratitude; too cute to shout to God in praise; too intelligent to say "Thank You"; and too dignified to say "Hallelujah"!

Let's examine portions of God's Word and see what praise and a thankful heart have to do with your promotion from the wilderness into a divine vision and into highest victory in Jesus Christ!

I am excited about praise! Praise for me is giving God all, and I have come to recognize that when you give God your *all*, all is what God will give to you! Enjoy this praise script and praise God! Hallelujah!

Bishop Larry D. Trotter

The Wilderness
(1) Place of wandering
(2) Place of rebellion
(3) Is a period in our lives
(4) The Wilderness is on our way to victory.

1
The Wilderness Days

Praise has become the intimate vehicle through which we are able to communicate with our awesome God. In my personal life, praise relinquishes me from burdens, confusion and foolishness.

As I have traveled across the country, I have encountered many of the saints who have been held hostage by depression, oppression and suppression of the enemy. I have recommended only one remedy to them and I offer it to you. It is simply *praise*! Praise is always the tool for defeating the attack of the enemy.

Praise has become the vehicle in my life that lifts heaviness. It has been my experience as I travel, preach and teach the Gospel of Jesus Christ that I encounter many people entrapped by situations and circumstances. These issues, great or small, that have held these precious people hostage, could all be eliminated through praise.

When I was a child growing up in the inner city of Chicago, I used to hear a story of a mother praising God for an hour in prayer and then making her request known in one minute. The story goes on to say that this mother would praise God in her prayer by saying to God, "God, I praise You for Your excellent greatness. I praise You for Your mighty acts and deeds. I praise You, God, for Your protection, guidance and deliverance. I praise You, God, for being a good God, all powerful, all knowing and all loving."

This mother would praise God by telling Him how excellent He is, then after fifty-nine minutes of boosting God's "ego," she would spend one minute asking God for whatever she needed.

One day, one of the children asked their mother why she spent fifty-nine minutes praising God and only one minute asking for what she needed. The mother's response was simple. She said that if she told God how great He was for fifty-nine minutes through praise, then He would have to give her whatever she asked for in her one-minute request.

If we just praise God, He will surely give us the desires of our hearts.

Life brings many ups and downs. Many of us have experienced, are experiencing, or will experience a point in our lives that can only be entitled "wilderness." The word *wilderness* means "a land not suited for farming; a land too dry, too rough, or too rocky to be cultivated, but sufficient for graving; desert." For many of us, the wilderness is an unfamiliar land, a place that presents situations and circumstances that only God can resolve for us. The wilderness is a period in our lives that seems to have constant unrest, just "one thing after another." The wilderness holds us captive in bondage until we find our way out.

In the pages ahead, I want to begin to examine the darkness of a wilderness experience. These wilderness days are biblically traced to the Israelites. The Israelites found themselves entangled as a nation in the wilderness. Ultimately, the release from the wilderness landed them in the promised land. The key for you to know as you read these anointed pages is, the Israelites made it out of the wilderness and so can you.

It is my desire that you understand that God has equipped us with tools that will deliver us and protect us in our wilderness experience. Our Christian survival tactic, our wilderness straight edge against the enemy, our wilderness compass, is PRAISE!

The Wilderness Days

The Israelites' journey begins when...

6 The Lord our God spake unto us in Horeb, saying, Ye have dwelt long enough in this mount:

7 Turn you, and take your journey, and go to the mount of the Amorites, and unto all the places nigh thereunto, in the plain, in the hills, and in the vale, and in the south, and by the sea side, to the land of the Canaanites, and unto Lebanon, unto the great river, the river Euphrates.

8 Behold, I have set the land before you: go in and possess the land which the Lord sware unto your fathers, Abraham, Isaac, and Jacob, to give unto them and to their seed after them.

9 And I spake unto you at that time, saying, I am not able to bear you myself alone:

10 The Lord your God hath multiplied you, and, behold, ye are this day as the stars of heaven for multitude.

11 (The Lord God of your fathers make you a thousand times so many more as ye are, and bless you, as he hath promised you!)

12 How can I myself alone bear your cumbrance, and your burden, and your strife?

13 Take you wise men, and understanding, and known among your tribes, and I will make them rulers over you.

14 And ye answered me, and said, The thing which thou hast spoken is good for us to do.

15 So I took the chief of your tribes, wise men, and known, and made them heads over you, captains over thousands, and captains over hundreds, and captains over fifties, and captains over tens, and officers among your tribes.

16 And I charged your judges at that time, saying, Hear the causes between your brethren, and judge righteously between every man and his brother, and the stranger that is with him.

17   Ye shall not respect persons in judgment; but ye shall hear the small as well as the great; ye shall not be afraid of the face of man; for the judgment is God's: and the cause that is too hard for you, bring it unto me, and I will hear it.

18   And I commanded you at that time all the things which ye should do.

19   And when we departed from Horeb, we went through all that great and terrible wilderness, which ye saw by the way of the mountain of the Amorites, as the Lord our God commanded us; and we came to Kadesh-barnea.

20   And I said unto you, Ye are come unto the mountain of the Amorites, which the Lord our God doth give unto us.

21   Behold, the Lord thy God hath set the land before thee: go up and possess it, as the Lord God of thy fathers hath said unto thee; fear not, neither be discouraged.

Deuteronomy 1:6-21

Although God was with the Israelites, God did not allow them to go around the wilderness but *through* the wilderness. God never *forsook* the Israelites! God takes us through situations so that we are able to praise Him for His deliverance. We are protected by divine love.

As a young boy in my mother's house, I remember the opening and closing of the soap opera, "As the World Turns." A replica of the earth turning on her axis was shown in the introduction and in the closing of the program, suggesting that another episode had begun and ended in the life of the actors and actresses.

Every week I still see the world turning — not on television introducing a soap opera, but introducing another page of my life as I pastor the people of God.

• As the world turns, more people are being killed needlessly each day.

- As the world turns, families are being ripped apart and children are raising themselves.
- As the world turns, children are being abducted or killed.
- As the world turns, churches are doing more inner fighting than outreach ministry.
- As the world turns, **The harvest is past, the summer is ended, and we are not saved** (Jeremiah 8:20).
- As the world turns, people are still doing their own thing in spite of what they hear through the Word of the Lord.

The more I examined the world turning around me, I began to be convicted of my ministry to help the hurting and rescue the lost. We are a people who are under mandate by God to minister to the world around us and in doing so, we are able to be the rescue ambassadors of the Lord.

Every man or woman of God must have a clear mandate of their ministry call. Personally, I was born to help deliver and lead people from where they are to where God desires them to be. I understand without a doubt that I am assigned to lead the people of Sweet Holy Spirit and vicinity into their own personal "promised land." I know that the common denominator of all my preaching is built around the theme, "From vision to victory."

But I also understand:

- Before every rainbow there is a storm.
- Before every mountain top there is a valley.
- Before every morning there is a midnight.
- Before every celebration there are some dark days.
- Before every crown there is a cross.
- Before there is gain there is pain.
- Before every promised land there is a wilderness.

Reality in every life is, rain may fall, the valley may run dry, morning may never seem to come. Whatever the situation or circumstance may be, God has not forgotten you.

It's not that God has forgotten you. It's not that you are not going to make it. It's not that everything around you is really failing. It's not that you are really going to lose. What's happening to you and me is, we are experiencing wilderness days.

The wilderness is a time no one really enjoys. There are days of difficulty, drought, loneliness, dilemmas, confusion, darkness and wanderings.

The children of Israel are a model from which we can learn — both good and bad.

Exodus 8:28 says, **And Pharaoh said, I will let you go, that ye may sacrifice to the Lord your God in the wilderness; only ye shall not go very far away: intreat for me.**

Exodus 13:18,20 says:

18 But God led the people about, through the way of the wilderness of the Red sea: and the children of Israel went up harnessed out of the land of Egypt.

20 And they took their journey from Succoth, and encamped in Etham, in the edge of the wilderness.

Exodus 14:3 says, **For Pharaoh will say of the children of Israel, they are entangled in the land, the wilderness hath shut them in.**

The Israelites had been delivered from Egypt and were headed for the "promised land," but they spent time in the wilderness.

Exodus 14:11,12 says:

11 And they said unto Moses, Because there were no graves in Egypt, hast thou taken us away to die in the wilderness? wherefore hast thou dealt thus with us, to carry us forth out of Egypt?

12 Is not this the word that we did tell thee in Egypt, saying, Let us alone, that we may serve the

Egyptians? For it had been better for us to serve the Egyptians, than that we should die in the wilderness.

John the Baptist preached in the wilderness of Judea. Jesus was in the wilderness when He was tempted by the devil. The children of Israel wandered in the wilderness.

The time period of the activities of the Israelite tribes between their departure from Egypt under Moses' leadership and when they were encamped by the Jordan River, ready to be led into Canaan by Joshua, was *forty years*.

The Israelite journeys are commonly known as "wilderness wanderings." In order to understand the nature of the wanderings, it is important to realize the difference between a wilderness and a desert. A desert is best imagined as a barren expanse of sand dunes or a rocky area that does not support any vegetation. Although a wilderness may also have barren areas, it has grassy upland plains, oases, springs and vegetation, such as flowers, shrubs and trees that can support many types of animal life.

Nothing seemed to stop the dissatisfaction among the wandering Israelites as they traveled toward Kadesh-barnea. Kadesh-barnea was on the southern frontier of Canaan. This is the place where the Israelites encamped after they left Egypt. Kadesh-barnea was the principal camp of the wilderness where the Israelites remained for forty years.

While in the wilderness, the Israelites complained about the lack of food. Even when God provided manna, they soon began to dislike it. God sent a flock of quail for food, which made the people ill and caused many deaths. (Numbers 11:32,33.) They had wilderness days on their way to victory, just as we will have some wilderness days on our way to victory.

Wilderness is a place of loneliness. It is an uninhabited, desolate place. On the way to your promised land, there will be desolate days, stormy days and some lonely days. There will be days of traveling where no one else has traveled.

Moving on to Victory

Here are some guidelines for moving *through* your wilderness to victory.

First, *keep your heart focused.* Paul gave us an admonition in this regard in Colossians 3:1,2:

1 If ye then be risen with Christ, *seek those things which are above,* **where Christ sitteth on the right hand of God.**

2 *Set your affection on things above,* **not on things on the earth.**

It's hard to think of water when you are in a dry place. It's hard to think of wealth when your bills are due. It is hard to think of peace when there is confusion all around you. It is hard to think of deliverance when it's obvious that you are being held hostage.

Keep your focus on Jesus, because **God is faithful, [He] will not suffer you to be tempted above that ye are able** (1 Corinthians 10:13).

Keep your focus on Jesus, even when you must deal with enemies, because you have God's promise for the destiny of the wicked:

1 Fret not thyself because of evildoers, neither be thou envious against the workers of iniquity.

2 For they shall soon be cut down like the grass, and wither as the green herb.

Psalm 37:1,2

Keep your focus on Jesus, because in the natural, there will be times when you will feel that you have lost your direction, gotten off track, goofed and made a wrong turn. Sand seems to have gotten in your eyes, and you can't get yourself together. But stay focused, remembering Romans 8:28: **And we know that all things work together for the good of them that love God, to them who are the called according to his purpose.**

If you don't stay focused, you will keep on wandering, you will miss your exodus, or you will tire out quickly.

A man who is running a marathon doesn't waver to the right or to the left, thinking about how he is feeling or what is going on. He doesn't have time to concern himself with who is running and who is not running. He has his heart and mind focused on the finish line. That's the way to live in the wilderness. Keep your heart and soul focused on the fact that you are coming out!

Second, *watch out for traps*. In every wilderness there will be some traps. On every journey there will be some surprises. In every person's life there will be some unexpected happenings.

If I can use my sanctified imagination, the Israelites who were in the wilderness for forty years didn't have regular checkups. They did not have the advantage of HMO, so one of the traps they ran into in the wilderness was sickness and disease. Others suffered fatigue. In the wilderness, it is more likely that you will become exhausted quickly. Your exhaustion in the wilderness will be due in part to a lack of food and fresh water. You will reach a burnout point. When you get tired, you will not be able to tolerate any foolishness. The wilderness will put your nerves on edge. It will make you impatient and waiting to explode.

After trying to be a Pastor every day, a Bible Teacher, a Community Leader, a Humanitarian, a Bishop of the Midwest Region, a good husband and a daddy, there are days I'm not the best to be around! That doesn't mean I'm not saved, that I lost my joy for God or family. It simply means *I am tired*. It's one of the traps in the wilderness that get to some of us!

Some of the children of Israel and some of us have been wandering so long in our wilderness that we are plagued with *sunstroke*. When you have sunstroke, you don't see straight, you don't hear well, you begin to act "off" and your knees get a little weak. That's the problem with some of the saints. We have been in the wilderness so long that we are feeling the effects of *sunstroke*!

The most serious of the wilderness traps is paralysis. In doing some research, I found that paralysis comes when the body stops receiving instructions from the brain. In other words, when the arms don't receive a signal from the brain, they won't function. When the legs don't receive instructions from the brain, they won't function. When the heart doesn't receive its orders from the brain, it won't pump.

When the people of God in or out of the wilderness refuse to receive instruction from the Head, then the Church becomes paralyzed.

Now, you must understand that the wilderness was not designed to kill you; it was not designed to hurt you; it was not designed to cripple you. Paralysis occurs when you don't hear God.

Whether you understand the wilderness or not, God must be praised! Praise in the wilderness will keep you from getting paralyzed. Praise in essence becomes your sunscreen, protection against paralysis and sunstroke. Praise is your energizer in the wilderness. One of the greatest traps of the enemy is that while you are going through, he tries to convince you that there is nothing to shout about.

Hear me and hear me good: *Praise is always in order, even in the wilderness!*

I believe you are at your Kadesh-barnea right now. Your wilderness days are coming to an end. If you can see beyond your present situation, beyond the sunstroke and through the "thicket," you are almost there. It is time to encourage yourself in the Lord! Tell yourself, "*It won't always be like this. My God shall supply all of my needs. The earth is still the Lord's. I am God's child and because of who I am, I am going to have what He wants me to have. I'm getting out of this wilderness. There is a better place for me.*"

Jesus experienced the wilderness, but He came out into a place of absolute victory. He was tempted of the devil for forty days and forty nights, but He overcame the devil by quoting, It is **written**, followed by a specific Scripture promise. Matthew 4:11 says, **Then the devil leaveth him, and, behold, angels came and ministered unto him**. Then began Jesus' three years of ministry.

In the following chapter, we will examine what praise has to do with receiving God's "best" blessings!

2
Praise — God's Channel of Blessings

1 O give thanks unto the Lord, for he is good: for his mercy endureth for ever.

2 Let the redeemed of the Lord say so, whom he hath redeemed from the hand of the enemy.

Psalm 107:1,2

For a long time, Christian people, particularly those of us of color, have been looked upon strangely for the way we worship the Lord. We have been called ignorant or unlearned because we "get happy." To those unfamiliar with true praise, this has been viewed as abnormal praise.

When we clap our hands unto the Lord, it has been interpreted as coming from our African heritage, being a rhythmatic people.

When we shout, some people have said, "It doesn't take all of that." In other words, we have been mocked because of some of our expressions of love and adoration for the Lord.

As believers in Jesus Christ, we are saints of God who assemble together in a place for worship. We, the people, are the church. Once we are caught up in real praise, people will be waiting in line to get into our churches, because praise is our channel of blessings.

Let's look through some "windows" that will help us to better understand praise — what it is and why it is our channel for receiving God's blessings.

Window #1

Man is dichotomous in nature: We are flesh and spirit; body and soul; carnal and spiritual; the old me and the new me. There are two worlds: This world and heaven where the throne of God is located. There are two realms: The natural and the spiritual.

When John was on the Isle of Patmos after writing seven letters to the seven churches and ending chapter 3 of the book of Revelation, in a letter to the church of Laodicea, he said, **He that hath an ear, let him hear what the Spirit saith unto the churches** (v. 22). Then he opens chapter 4 by saying:

1   After this I looked, and, behold, a door was opened in heaven: and the first voice which I heard was as it were of a trumpet talking with me; which said, Come up hither, and I will shew thee things which must be hereafter.

2   And immediately I was in the spirit: and, behold, a throne was set in heaven, and one sat on the throne.

3   And he that sat was to look upon like a jasper and a sardine stone: and there was a rainbow round about the throne, in sight like unto an emerald.

4   And round about the throne were four and twenty seats: and upon the seats I saw four and twenty elders sitting, clothed in white raiment; and they had on their heads crowns of gold.

5   And out of the throne proceeded lightnings and thunderings and voices: and there were seven lamps of fire burning before the throne, which are the seven Spirits of God.

6   And before the throne there was a sea of glass like unto crystal: and in the midst of the throne, and round about the throne, were four beasts full of eyes before and behind.

7   And the first beast was like a lion, and the second beast like a calf, and the third beast

had a face as a man, and the fourth beast was like a flying eagle.

8   And the four beasts had each of them six wings about him; and they were full of eyes within: and they rest not day and night, saying, Holy, holy, holy, Lord God Almighty, which was, and is, and is to come...

11   Thou art worthy, O Lord, to receive glory and honour and power: for thou hast created all things, and for thy pleasure they are and were created.

Verses 1-8,11

If anybody should have been down, sad, or disgusted, it should have been John. He had been cast alone on this island, which was one world. But in the other world, there was a rainbow, jewels and a heavenly sight where praise went forth.

Praise can take you from the things that you know are real — the bills, sickness, death, fear, doubt, rejection, anxiety, wars and rumors of war — to another world, another realm of reality, another level of spirituality, the heavenly, the eternal.

Jesus said to John, **Come up hither**, which means, "Come up higher." The door is open. I'm still on the throne. I'm yet in control. All power is Mine."

There was identification. He recognized the voice. There was an invitation, **Come up higher**. There was a proclamation: "Things are not like they appear. Things are not out of control. You're not in the wrong world. The devil has not won. Evil has not triumphed. Man is not a victim of cruel choice. We are not living on a ball that's getting ready to explode."

Praise ushers us into God's presence. When we see God as He is, we will praise Him as we ought. Praise is nothing more or less than a commitment to and a confession of the sovereign power and providence of God.

The absence of praise simply means that someone has an inadequate view of God. To know Him *is* to praise Him. That's the right perspective.

Window #2

Praise was written from the "beginning" of everything! Job 38:7 says, **When the morning stars sang together, and all the sons of God shouted for joy.**

The earth was girded in praise: The stars sang, the heavenly bodies rejoiced and the angels shouted. Praise filled the world in the days of its beginnings. Everything that was created joined in the chorus of praise.

Everything was made *to praise the Lord*. Isaiah 43:21 says, **This people have I formed for myself;** *they shall shew forth my praise.* We were created to praise the Lord.

In Psalm 148, every created thing is commanded to praise the Lord:

    1   Praise ye the Lord. Praise ye the Lord from the heavens: praise him in the heights.

    2   Praise ye him, all his angels: praise ye him, all his hosts.

    3   Praise ye him, sun and moon: praise him, all ye stars of light.

    4   Praise him, ye heavens of heavens, and ye waters that be above the heavens.

    5   Let them praise the name of the Lord: for he commanded, and they were created.

    6   He hath also stablished them for ever and ever: he hath made a decree which shall not pass.

    7   Praise the Lord from the earth, ye dragons, and all deeps:

    8   Fire, and hail; snow, and vapour; stormy wind fulfilling his word:

    9   Mountains, and all hills; fruitful trees, and all cedars:

10   Beasts, and all cattle; creeping things, and flying fowl:

11   Kings of the earth, and all people; princes and all judges of the earth:

12   Both young men, and maidens; old men, and children:

13   Let them praise the name of the Lord: for his name alone is excellent; his glory is above the earth and heaven.

14   He also exalteth the horn of his people, the praise of all his saints; even the children of Israel, a people near unto him. Praise ye the Lord.

Verses 1-14

Jesus said, **I tell you that, if these** [the disciples, including you and me] **should hold their peace, the stones would immediately cry out** (Luke 19:40).

I say:

- Let the bees buzz His praise.
- Let the cattle low it.
- Let the dogs bark it.
- Let the cats meow it.
- Let the snakes hiss it.
- Let the frogs hop it.
- Let the wolves howl it.

Let everything that has breath praise the Lord!

Window #3

Praise is where God lives. Psalm 22:3 says, **But thou art holy, O thou that inhabitest the praises of Israel.**

Praise is a permanent address! God is at home in an atmosphere of praise.

Psalm 48:1 says, **Great is the Lord, and greatly to be praised.**

I dare you to stop your crying and begging and begin to praise the Lord. Healing comes on the wings of praise. Emotions are stabilized during praise. The entire demeanor of a person changes when he or she becomes a praise person.

While God is omnipresent — everywhere at the same time — He is not manifested everywhere. But He will manifest where praise has created an atmosphere for Him to be at home!

Window #4

Praise is a lethal weapon to the believer.

The word *praise* in Psalm 8:2, translated from the original text, means "strength."

> 2   Out of the mouth of babes and sucklings hast thou ordained strength because of thine enemies, that thou mightest still the enemy and the avenger.

God appoints praise, because it stops the devil in his tracks. Neither the devil nor his demons can offer any protest in an atmosphere of praise. When they fell from grace, they could no longer handle a heavenly atmosphere. When drums go to beating or when saints go to dancing in praise to God, the devil takes off!

In the next chapter we will attempt to better understand the various types of praise.

3
Understanding Praise

1   I will praise thee with my whole heart: before the gods will I sing praise unto thee.

2   I will worship toward thy holy temple, and praise thy name for thy lovingkindness and for thy truth: for thou hast magnified thy word above all thy name.

3   In the day when I cried thou answeredst me, and strengthenedst me with strength in my soul.

Psalm 138:1-3

Here are four descriptions of what praise should be:

1. *Praise must be Christ-centered.*

Any saint who wants to be successful must have Christ at the center of his life. A person without Christ is like:

- A plant without sunshine.
- Sugar without sweetening.
- Bread without butter.
- Chitterlings without hot sauce.

Praise is not a state of art. *It is a state of the heart.* By the state of the heart I mean the driving force behind the worship life of the believer.

Deuteronomy 6:5 says, **And thou shalt love the Lord thy God with all thine heart, and with all thy soul, and with all thy might.**

First Samuel 16:7 says, **Man looketh on the outward appearance, but the Lord looketh on the heart.**

Psalm 51:10 says, **Create in me a clean heart, O God; and renew a right spirit within me.**

2. *Praise must be sensible.*

If you know the Lord and you acknowledge Him daily, then your praise will be sincere.

We have no problem jumping and hollering at our favorite athletic events, so it makes good sense that we ought to praise the God of our salvation.

Praise must be sensible. God is a God of order, so everything we do, we ought to be able to explain so that even unbelievers and the people who are not committed to praise will desire to get involved. Sensible praise produces a balanced appeal to mind, heart and spirit.

The late William Temple, Archbishop of Canterbury, once wrote that praise is the submission of all our nature to God.

Praise is the quickening of the conscience by His holiness; the nourishment of the mind with His truth; the purifying of imagination by His beauty; the opening of the heart to His love; and the surrender of the will to His purposes.

3. *Praise must be Spirit led.*

Jesus said, **God is a Spirit: and they that worship him must worship him in spirit and in truth** (John 4:24).

I don't know about you, but I am born of the Spirit; anointed and appointed by the Spirit; chosen by the Spirit; ordained by the Spirit; named by the Spirit; led by the Spirit; a disciple of the Spirit; lifted by the Spirit; gifted by the Spirit; and I praise in the Spirit!

4. *Praise must be sacrificial.*

We must be willing to sacrifice our time, energy, pride, prudence, position, possessions, words and conversations

Understanding Praise

and totally involve ourselves in praise.

Some of the Greek and Hebrew words for praise stress the intimacy and intensity of the praise cycle.

Hallal, which is the prefix of the word *hallelujah*, means "to boast, brag, rave, celebrate even to the point of looking foolish." It is a word for praise that invites God in and drives Satan out.

Yadah means "the lifting of the hands in praise." For a long time many people were hesitant to lift their hands in praise and worship because they didn't want to be identified as a charismatic or a holy roller.

Eusebo means "the waving of the hands in praise."

Barak means "to bless or congratulate God; to applaud." It is customary, kind and courteous when someone gives a great performance that those who are watching put their hands together and barak or applaud that individual. Surely God has and is yet giving us a great performance and is worthy of our praise!

Tehilliah means "to sing aloud, sound a hymn, call and response." For example:

Hallelujah — Hallelujah!

Praise the Lord — Praise the Lord!

Glory to God! — Glory to God!

Zamar is "the use of music in praise." We use the piano, the organ, drums, tambourines and cymbals — all kinds of instrumentation.

Todah means "to extend the hands in thanksgiving, cupped to receive."

Gil means "to shout, circle in joy."

Pazaz means "to leap for joy."

Doxa means "to glorify."

The final and most powerful word to me in the activity of praise, other than hallelujah, is *Shabach*, which means "to commence; to make a long, loud noise unto the Lord; to overextend yourself in praise to the Lord; give it all to Him, just like Jacob wrestling with the angel, or David dancing before the Lord until his royal robe fell off."

In the next chapter, we will look at the role of praise in "getting through your mess"!!

4
How To Make It Through Your Mess

Satan can't stand people who praise God; neither can he stand a praise atmosphere.

Have you ever been in a mess? a fix? a jam? a pickle? a jumble? between the devil and the deep sea? between a rock and a hard place? at the end of your rope?

Praise will cause you to reach beyond your situations and circumstances. It is a channel of God's blessings, but it is also a means of deliverance out of your messes. All of them!

The story of Jehoshaphat is an excellent example of being in a *mess*.

> 12 O our God, wilt thou not judge them? for we have no might against this great company that cometh against us; neither know we what to do: but our eyes are upon thee.
>
> 13 And all Judah stood before the Lord, with their little ones, their wives, and their children.
>
> 14 Then upon Jahaziel the son of Zechariah, the son of Benaiah, the son of Jeiel, the son of Mattaniah, a Levite of the sons of Asaph, came the Spirit of the Lord in the midst of the congregation;
>
> 15 And he said, Hearken ye, all Judah, and ye inhabitants of Jerusalem, and thou king Jehoshaphat, Thus saith the Lord unto you, Be not afraid nor dismayed by reason of this great multitude; for the battle is not yours, but God's.

16   To morrow go ye down against them: behold, they come up by the cliff of Ziz; and ye shall find them at the end of the brook, before the wilderness of Jeruel.

17   Ye shall not need to fight in this battle: set yourselves, stand ye still, and see the salvation of the Lord with you, O Judah and Jerusalem: fear not, nor be dismayed; to morrow go out against them: for the Lord will be with you.

18   And Jehoshaphat bowed his head with his face to the ground: and all Judah and the inhabitants of Jerusalem fell before the Lord, worshipping the Lord.

19   And the Levites, of the children of the Kohathites, and of the children of the Korhites, stood up to praise the Lord God of Israel with a loud voice on high.

20   And they rose early in the morning, and went forth into the wilderness of Tekoa: and as they went forth, Jehoshaphat stood and said, Hear me, O Judah, and ye inhabitants of Jerusalem; Believe in the Lord your God, so shall ye be established; believe his prophets, so shall ye prosper.

21   And when he had consulted with the people, he appointed singers unto the Lord, and that should praise the beauty of holiness, as they went out before the army, and to say, Praise the Lord; for his mercy endureth for ever.

22   And when they began to sing and to praise, the Lord set ambushments against the children of Ammon, Moab, and mount Seir, which were come against Judah; and they were smitten.

Here are seven steps to take you through your messes:

1. *Praise is private.*

Jehoshaphat was in a mess. He had married the wrong woman. The enemy was on his way to get him and his people. Jehoshaphat called the people together and his first words were to God — not to the people. It was private and personal.

Jehoshaphat is reminded of God's position. He recounts what God has done in the past. He rests on God's power in the privacy of praise. Like Jehoshaphat, we need to realize who God is and thank Him. We need to remember what He has done and thank Him. We need to praise Him for what He will do in the future.

2. *If you want to step through your mess, start at the point of the problem.*

Jehoshaphat didn't make light of the situation he was in. His situation was a mess and he called it just that. He didn't coat it with superficial slang. He didn't laugh it off. He didn't throw a pity party. He admitted it to God and then pulled himself together.

3. *To step through your mess, cease to trust in your flesh.*

Jehoshaphat said, "We have no power. We don't know what to do." There is nothing wrong with admitting weakness. Some people say that mature men and women don't admit weakness. Hogwash!

Praise is a death blow to the flesh. In the flesh, we will be concerned about what our friends think, how our clothes look and how we will be perceived. But praise is a denial of self-trust, pride and independence. When Jehoshaphat admitted, "We have no power, and we don't know what to do," he moved from the natural to the spiritual realm.

Zechariah 4:6 says, **Not by might, nor by power, but by my spirit, saith the Lord of hosts**. We cannot trust in the flesh.

4. *To step through your mess, keep your mind fully concentrated on God.*

The last words of Jehoshaphat's prayer were, **Neither know we what to do: but our eyes are upon thee** (2 Chronicles 20:12).

Be determined to wait on God and keep your focus on Him until His next directive comes.

5. *Remain before God.*

Second Chronicles 20:13 says, **And all Judah stood before the Lord, with their little ones, their wives, and their children**. *Waiting* is part of the mood of praise. This is a time of meditation, investigation, cleansing and consecration.

6. *Confess the truth of God.*

In Jehoshaphat's situation, God said, **Be not afraid nor dismayed by reason of this great multitude; for the battle is not yours, but God's** (v. 15). Then God told Jehoshaphat and his troops exactly where the enemy would be.

> **16 To morrow go ye down against them: behold, they come up by the cliff of Ziz; and ye shall find them at the end of the brook, before the wilderness of Jeruel.**
>
> **17 Ye shall not need to fight in this battle: set yourselves, stand ye still, and see the salvation of the Lord with you, O Judah and Jerusalem: fear not, nor be dismayed; to morrow go out against them: for the Lord will be with you.**
>
> **Verses 16,17**

So what did Jehoshaphat and his troops do? **They fell before the Lord,** *worshipping the Lord.* And they stood up to *praise the Lord God of Israel* **with a loud voice on high** (vv. 18,19).

The next morning Jehoshaphat spoke to all of his troops: **Hear me, O Judah, and ye inhabitants of Jerusalem; Believe in the Lord your God, so shall ye be established; believe his prophets, so shall ye prosper** (v. 20).

The rejoicing on the part of Jehoshaphat and all Judah and Jerusalem revealed their complete trust in a God of truth.

7. *To get through your mess, be committed to obey.*

Verses 21 and 22 say that Jehoshaphat **appointed sing-**

ers unto the Lord, and that should praise the beauty of holiness, as they went out before the army, and to say, Praise the Lord; for his mercy endureth for ever. And when they began to sing and to praise, the Lord set ambushments against the children of Ammon, Moab, and mount Seir, which were come against Judah; and they were smitten.

Because of their obedience to the word of the Lord, their enemies were defeated. The enemy army was completely annihilated as they turned on each other. Verse 24 says of the enemy army, **None escaped**.

Collecting Enemy Spoils

It took Jehoshaphat and his army three days to gather the spoils of the enemy. Verses 26-29 say:

> **26** And on the fourth day they assembled themselves in the valley of Berachah; for there they blessed the Lord: therefore the name of the same place was called, The valley of Berachah, unto this day.
>
> **27** Then they returned, every man of Judah and Jerusalem, and Jehoshaphat in the forefront of them, to go again to Jerusalem with joy; for the Lord had made them to rejoice over their enemies.
>
> **28** And they came to Jerusalem with psalteries and harps and trumpets unto the house of the Lord.
>
> **29** And the fear of God was on all the kingdoms of those countries, when they had heard that the Lord fought against the enemies of Israel.

These same steps will bring you through your mess into victory! Praise is the key!

God has a way, through "praise," of allowing us to become the victors rather than the victims. Your enemy has many things that will become yours as you submit to God through praise.

In the next chapter, we'll talk about the meaning of the word *hallelujah* and its role in praise.

5
What About "Hallelujah"?

1   And after these things I heard a great voice of much people in heaven, saying, Alleluia; Salvation, and glory, and honour, and power unto the Lord our God:

3   And again they said, Alleluia. And her smoke rose up for ever and ever.

4   And the four and twenty elders and the four beasts fell down and worshipped God that sat on the throne, saying, Amen; Alleluia.

6   And I heard as it were the voice of a great multitude, and as the voice of many waters, and as the voice of mighty thunderings, saying, Alleluia: for the Lord God omnipotent reigneth.

Revelation 19:1,3,4,6

As Jesus entered the holy city of Jerusalem for the last time before His crucifixion, some of the people spread their garments before Him; others waved branches of trees at Him, laying them in His path; and many shouted, *"Hosanna."* (Mark 11:9.)

Hosanna in the Greek means "to save or help now." But in the Hebrew it means "Hallelujah."

Rarely do you see a church scene in a play where someone doesn't shout *hallelujah* at some point. Never have I seen the Christmas holiday come and go without hearing some carols say *hallelujah*.

You will never attend a "Praise God" church without someone in the congregation hollering *hallelujah*.

The word *hallelujah* means more than you can imagine. It has such majesty and completeness. Instead of being translated, it was transliterated. It is the only word that no matter where you go on the face of the earth, the pronunciation remains the same.

Hallelujah actually is a combination of two Hebrew words: *Hallal*, which means "to boast; to brag on; to praise; to make a show of, even to the point of looking foolish." *Jah* is the shortened name for Jehovah God. When you add "u" in the middle, the word *hallelujah* becomes the spontaneous outcry of those who are excited about God!

Are you excited about God? Are you excited about what He has done? Are you excited about what He is doing and what He is going to do? Tell Him, *hallelujah*! It is the exclamation of one who is conscious of the majesty of God. Thus, *hallelujah* is the highest praise that anyone can give to God!

Hallelujah (alleluia), "Praise ye the Lord," or "Praise the Lord" is found in the Bible twenty-nine times: Twenty-five times in the psalms and four times in Revelation 19.

Somewhere in each day, we should utter to God our highest praise — magnificent, complete, serious and ultimate praise. *Hallelujah* is the word we can use to convey this meaning.

Hallelujah has a ring of purpose. It is both God's purpose and His providence that all creation praise Him!

Psalm 150:6 says, **Let every thing that hath breath praise the Lord**. In one word, one language, one tongue, one heart, one body and one soul, people are praising with the word *hallelujah*! The basic purpose of praising God is that He inhabits it, He enjoys it and He requires it.

Hallelujah has a ring of power to it. The Greek word for *power* is "dunamis." Through the hallelujah psalms, there is a constant sound of God's might and ability.

Psalm 106:2 says, **Who can utter the mighty acts of the Lord? who can shew forth all his praise?**

In our text from Revelation 19, verse 1 says, **Alleluia; Salvation, and glory, and honour, and** *power*, **unto the Lord our God.** Verse 6 says, **Alleluia: for the Lord God omnipotent reigneth.**

Hallelujah seems to be the only reasonable response we can give in light of God's greatness. The crescendo continues to rise in Psalm 150:2: **Praise him for his mighty acts: praise him according to his excellent greatness.**

One of the greatest hymns of the Church, "How Great Thou Art," speaks of God's power to the fullest.

The hallelujah of redemption is crowned, because it has the ring of power. The hallelujah of retribution is complete, because it has the ring of power. The hallelujah of reign is confirmed, because it has the ring of power. The hallelujah of relationship is consummated, because it has the ring of power.

Hallelujah also has a ring of presence to it. In other words, in addition to giving praise to God, when you say it, you are inviting God to be present with you. If you just shout *Hallelujah*, you are calling God's presence in and running the devil out. This kind of praise drives Satan mad.

Most of us are familiar with the special musical masterpiece, "The Messiah." In 1741 George Frederick Handel was given a manuscript of poetic and scriptural excerpts from Charles Jenners entitled, "A Sacred Oratorio."

Handel was fifty-seven years old. His personal life was in bad shape; he was physically and emotionally sick; he was a manic depressive.

Handel shut himself in for about twenty-four days and composed the Messiah. As he read passages like, "He was despised and rejected of men," he would shout, *Hallelujah*! As he read, "His name shall be called Wonderful, Counselor, Mighty God, Everlasting Father," he would shout, *Hallelujah*! His soul began to be revived and history tells us that he often lifted his hands until he finished the *Hallelujah* chorus.

At the first major performance of "The Messiah," the king was so moved by the last chorus, he stood and all the people stood with him. Even today in concert halls all across the country, when the last chorus is sung, which says, "For He shall reign forever and ever," everyone stands.

If you want God's presence with you, use the word *hallelujah* often.

Hallelujah looks in all directions:

- Backwards to salvation commenced.
- Forward to salvation crowned.
- Upward to God enthroned.
- Downward to the devil in chains.
- Inward to fear diminished.
- Outward to faith established righteousness and readiness.

When you say *hallelujah*, God is glorified; saints are edified; lives are changed; burdens are lifted; temptations are overcome; needs are met; bodies are healed; souls are enriched.

When you say *hallelujah*, nerves are settled; differences are resolved; doubts are destroyed; fears are banished; hearts are touched; problems are solved; blessings are enjoyed.

When you say *hallelujah*, questions are answered; ministries are inspired; demons are overthrown; frustrations are abolished; emotions are stirred; confusion is cleared.

When you say *hallelujah*, minds are enlightened; sorrows are removed; sins are confessed; spirits are revived; joys are received; hopes are restored; decisions are made; angels are excited.

What do you need from God? Don't tell Him about your problems, your situations, or your burdens. Just say, *hallelujah*!

Hallelujah is the culmination of everything needed in the Christian pilgrimage. It is a word of power that gets the immediate attention of God.

Hallelujah! Let us examine the next chapter to find out how to praise through pressure.

6
Praise Your Way Through Pressure

> 6 Be careful for nothing; but in every thing by prayer and supplication with thanksgiving let your requests be made known unto God.
>
> 7 And the peace of God, which passeth all understanding, shall keep your hearts and minds through Christ Jesus.
>
> Philippians 4:6,7

Every person is faced with a multiplicity of problems, pressures and obstacles in this life. Sometimes adversities seem to be stacked in a line and one follows on the heels of another. The good news is, David the psalmist said, **Many are the afflictions of the righteous:** *but the Lord delivereth him out of them all* (Psalm 34:19).

Some people are quick to respond to a praise cure-all, "But you just don't know my situation. Pressures are all around me."

What is *pressure*? It is strain, stress, trouble, affliction, heaviness, distress, having a new car but no money for gas. *Pressure* also is:

• Dressing up to go out, clean as the board of health, and your little brother, sister, or child smudges your attire with chocolate ice cream.

• Trying to quit smoking, while those working around you smoke constantly.

• You're starved, you spend your last money on something to eat, and when you get home everybody wants some!

- Mama told you to be home at 11:00 p.m. and Willie's old car breaks down.
- Trying to lose weight and people you hardly know keep inviting you to dinner.
- Buying a new wardrobe and everything is too tight.
- Studying for a test all night long only to find when you get to class, the teacher has postponed it.

There are all types of pressure. Sometimes pressures include failure, temptation, or disappointments. Whatever your pressure — financial, job, school, home, relationships — you can praise your way through it. Psalm 30:5 says, **Weeping may endure for a night, but joy cometh in the morning.**

While you are on your knees praying, God sends an angel and puts him on the run in your behalf. While you are still praying, the thing you are praying about is already done!

In everything, thank God. When depressed, thank God, not *for* the depression, but for the fact that He is the depression-lifter! When problems come, thank God. When you are thanking God, He is working it out. He is fixing the situation, While you are shouting *hallelujah*, victory is being completed. While you are singing glory, your answer is being manifested.

Remember these nine phrases:
- *Eternity* is the longest word.
- *Grace* is the sweetest word.
- *Hell* is the hottest word.
- *Peace* is the calmest word.
- *Lost* is the saddest word.
- *Death* is the coldest word.
- *Heaven* is the brightest word.
- *Love* is the broadest word.
- *Jesus* is the greatest word!

Let every thing that hath breath praise the Lord. Praise ye the Lord (Psalm 150:6).

The next chapter is a personal favorite. We will examine how to praise God through giving.

7

Praise Through Giving

> 6   But this I say, He which soweth sparingly shall reap also sparingly; and he which soweth bountifully shall reap also bountifully.
>
> 7   Every man according as he purposeth in his heart, so let him give; not grudgingly, or of necessity: for God loveth a cheerful giver.
>
> 2 Corinthians 9:6,7

True praise is accompanied by giving out of a cheerful heart.

God gave us His very best, first in the creation. He created the universe and all that is in it in six days. He made the redwood trees of California; the cashew trees of Africa; the palm trees of Florida; the polar bears of Alaska; the flowing canals of Belgium; and the snowy mountains of Switzerland.

God created man in His own image and likeness. The body is wonderfully constructed. God took some iron, sugar, salt, carbon, iodine, phosphorus, lime, calcium and some other materials. He gave us over 200 bones; 600 muscles; 970 miles of blood vessels; 400 cups on the tongue so we can taste the difference between sweet and bitter, hot and mild, or salty and sour; 2,000 hairs in our ears to tune in the sounds; 40 pounds of jaw pressure; ten million nerves and branches; 3,500 sweat tubes to each square inch of the skin; 20 million mouths to suck food through the intestines; 600 million air cells to the lungs that inhale 2,400 gallons of air daily; a telephone system that relates to the brain instantly any known sound, taste, sight, touch or smell; a heart that beats 4,200 times an hour and a heart that pumps 12 tons of blood each day. Then He blew into man the breath of life and man became a living soul.

Then Jesus died for man, arose for man and gave man a commandment, "Let everything that has breath praise Me."

If God did all of that for us, then how much do we owe Him? What can we render unto the Lord for all His benefits? What can we give a God Who has done so much for us? What is our obligation? What is our indebtedness?

The two areas I want us to look at are: 1) The giving of yourself; and 2) The giving of your substance.

Giving of Yourself

Praise is personal and it takes time and energy. You must be willing to give of yourself without a care as to what others think of you.

In giving of myself, I have learned that I am never finished. My ministry is a continuous cycle of assignments. When I complete one message, I start getting ready for another. When I visit the sick, I get ready to go visit another. When I witness to one person, here comes another. When I counsel one couple, here comes another couple. When I liquidate one problem or one bill, here comes another. My work is never done!

What good are you to the Kingdom of God if you never give of yourself?

Here are some areas where you can invest yourself in most churches:

- Tutor / Literacy Ministry
- Choir member / Music Ministry
- Office worker
- Computer operator
- Long-range planning committee

- Evangelism teams
- Distribution of food / Homeless Ministry
- Children's Ministry
- Usher / Ministry of Helps
- Orchestra
- Youth worker
- Men's Fellowship
- Women's Fellowship

And the list goes on. There is something each of us can do. Report for duty and give of yourself cheerfully!

Giving of Your Substance

Giving of your substance — your tithes and offerings — ought to be the high point of any worship service.

Proverbs 3:9,10 says:

9 Honour the Lord with thy substance, and with the firstfruits of all thine increase:

10 So shall thy barns be filled with plenty, and thy presses shall burst out with new wine.

I believe there should be a praise break at offering time, because we are praising God that we have something to give; and we are praising Him because we know it is right to tithe and give offerings.

It takes finances to run the church. It takes finances to burn the lights, to minister to the poor, to print tracts and bulletins, to make phone calls and to drive a car.

Malachi 3:8-10 says:

8 Will a man rob God? Yet ye have robbed me. But ye say, Wherein have we robbed thee? In tithes and offerings.

9 Ye are cursed with a curse: for ye have robbed me, even this whole nation.

> **10** Bring ye all the tithes into the storehouse, that there may be meat in mine house, and prove me now herewith, saith the Lord of hosts [here's the promise], **if I will not open you the windows of heaven, and pour you out a blessing, that there shall not be room enough to receive it.**

God's admonition through Malachi for tithing and giving offerings doesn't say, "Cook a chicken, have a rummage sale, or tip God." It says, **Bring ye all the tithes into the storehouse** (v. 10).

If you really want to be blessed, if you really want to praise God totally, if you really want the windows of heaven to be opened, bring your tithes and offerings! It shows recognition of God's sovereign ownership of everything. It is a reflection of your stewardship. Tithing is a command — not an option!

Giving is made better if it is done with an attitude of praise. As we give to God our talents, our time and our tithe, do it with a spirit of praise. Give all that you have to God, and watch Him multiply your blessings before your eyes. I am excited about your future because of your new commitment in giving.

In the next chapter, we will examine what comes after praise.

8
What Comes After Praise?

> 11 If any man speak, let him speak as the oracles of God; if any man minister, let him do it as of the ability which God giveth: that God in all things may be glorified through Jesus Christ, to whom be praise and dominion for ever and ever. Amen.
>
> 12 Beloved, think it not strange concerning the fiery trial which is to try you, as though some strange thing happened unto you:
>
> 13 But rejoice, inasmuch as ye are partakers of Christ's sufferings; that, when his glory shall be revealed, ye may be glad also with exceeding joy.
>
> 1 Peter 4:11-13

Jesus Christ never birthed a poor or dead church. He doesn't want poor giving, poor preaching, poor singing, poor planning, or poor teaching. And He certainly doesn't want poor praising. David the psalmist said that God inhabits our praises. (Psalm 22:3.)

Don't allow yourself to be lazy, laid back, lukewarm, lifeless, or lost, but get involved in praising the Lord.

What happens after the music stops? What should still be going on when the "praise break" is over? What comes after we have danced all night? What happens after the benediction? How shall we conduct ourselves after church?

1. *Trials often follow praise.*

The Bible makes it clear that some suffering is the result of evil action or sin. This type of suffering came upon man after the fall of Adam and Eve in the Garden of Eden. Some suffering, however, is not related to the past but is forward-looking in that it serves to shape and refine God's children.

> **6 Wherein ye greatly rejoice, though now for a season, if need be, ye are in heaviness through manifold temptations:**
>
> **7 That the trial of your faith, being much more precious than of gold that perisheth, though it be tried with fire, might be found unto praise and honour and glory at the appearing of Jesus Christ.**
>
> **1 Peter 1:6,7**

First Peter 5:10 says:

> **But the God of all grace, who hath called us unto his eternal glory by Christ Jesus, after that ye have suffered a while, make you perfect, stablish, strengthen, settle you.**

Paul speaks of the **fellowship of his** [Christ's] **sufferings** (Philippians 3:10). Believers share in the suffering of Christ in the sense that through suffering we *identify* with Him.

When the devil realizes that you are going to continue to give God glory, he will eventually move on.

2. *After praise there must be practice.*

There is no way that you can be in real praise to God and your lifestyle stays the same. There is something about praise that changes your attitude as it relates to holy living. Beloved, think it not strange that even through suffering, even after the "hype" of praise, you must not just talk the talk but you must walk the walk! There must be practice.

Paul said:

> **15 See then that ye walk circumspectly, not as fools, but as wise,**
>
> **16 Redeeming the time, because the days are evil.**
>
> **Ephesians 5:15,16**

Hebrews 12:14 says, **Follow peace with all men, and holiness, without which no man shall see the Lord.**

Real saints look like saints, they talk like saints, they act like saints and they walk like saints. David said, **Thy word have I hid in mine heart, that I might not sin against thee** (Psalm 119:11). You must have the Word in your heart to be able to practice praise.

In a game, the whole team gets excited about winning, but at some point there must be a "time out" so the players can receive instructions as to how best use the time that they have left. They want their efforts to be productive.

After the outpouring of the Spirit, after the praise break, there should be a time out to make sure that when the praise is over, some powerful, positive and productive things will result.

When you finish praising God, you will have a better attitude. When you finish shouting, you should be more obedient to your parents and those in authority over you. When you finish jumping, you should treat your spouse better. When you finish in the high praises of a service, you ought to complete school with better grades. When you finish in the praise service, you ought to be stronger and more productive.

When praises go up to God, His blessings come down — blessings of healing, holiness, abundance, obedience, strength and productivity.

When we finish praising, we have a life to live, people to bring to salvation and a job to do. There are hurting people who need our help. We have a prize to reach, a mountain to climb.

3. *After praise comes abundant joy.*

There is absolutely no way you can praise God and your demeanor remain the same. Praise creates an atmosphere of excitement. It births an ambiance of joy. It produces exaltation. When you praise God, you feel better, and you receive His abundance.

Joy is a positive attitude or pleasant emotion, or delight. Many levels of joy are described in the Bible, including gladness, contentment and cheerfulness. The joy which the people of God should have is holy and pure. This joy rises above circumstances and focuses on the very character of God.

The joy required by a righteous person is produced by the Spirit of God through a life of praise.

First Thessalonians 1:6 says, **And ye became followers of us, and of the Lord, having received the word in much affliction, with joy of the Holy Ghost.** First Thessalonians 3:9 says, **For what thanks can we render to God again for you, for all the joy wherewith we joy for your sakes before our God.**

> Joys are flowing like a river
> Since the Comforter has come.
> He abides with us forever,
> Makes a trusting heart His home.
>
> Blessed quietness, holy quietness,
> What assurance in my soul.
> On the stormy sea Jesus speaks to me,
> And the billow seems to roll.
>
> Like the rain that falls from heaven,
> Like the sunlight from the sky.
> So the Holy Ghost is given,
> Coming on us from on High.

17   **For the kingdom of God is not meat and drink; but righteousness, and peace, and joy in the Holy Ghost.**

18   **For he that in these things serveth Christ is acceptable to God, and approved of men.**

Romans 14:17,18

Isaiah said it this way: If you have a spirit of heaviness, try on the garment of praise. (Isaiah 61:3.) After praise comes joy! We have joy because:

- Our burdens have become blessings.
- Our shame has been turned to sunshine.
- Our darkness has been turned into morning.
- Our guilt has been washed away in Jesus' blood.
- Our torments have become triumphs.
- Our cares have been cast upon the Lord.
- Our heartaches have been turned to hallelujahs!

The more I praise Him, the better I'll act, the better I'll feel, the closer I'll get and the higher I'll go!

24 Now unto him that is able to keep you from falling, and to present you faultless before the presence of his glory with exceeding joy,

25 To the only wise God our Saviour, be glory and majesty, dominion and power, both now and ever. Amen.

Jude 24,25

9
Three-fold Blessing for Praisers

There is a three-fold blessing for praisers.

First, *they enjoy prominence.* They gain rulership. They overcome bitterness, anxiety and depression.

Luke 6:38 applies to every area of life, including the sacrifice of praise.

> **Give, and it shall be given unto you; good measure, pressed down, and shaken together, and running over, shall men give into your bosom. For with the same measure that ye mete withal it shall be measured to you again.**

Second, *praisers have open access to God's blessings.*

They receive answers to prayer; added strength, both individually and corporately; and protection. God responds to praise!

Third, *praisers continue as conquerors.*

Romans 8:37 says, **We are more than conquerors through him that loved us.**

As we praise, God fights our battles. He is in the ring, and all we have to do is be on the outside of the ring, saying, "Hallelujah! Glory to God! Praise the Lord! Thank You, Jesus!"

Exodus 14:13,14 says:

> **13 Fear ye not, stand still, and see the salvation of the Lord, which he will shew to you to day: for the**

Egyptians [a type of the enemy] whom ye have seen to day, ye shall see them again no more for ever.

14   The Lord shall fight for you, and ye shall hold your peace.

Praise God and get your three-fold blessing. You are entitled to it; God desires for you to have it; and you deserve it because you are His child.

How pure is your praise? The next chapter will let you know.

10

How Pure Is Your Praise?

> 12 On the next day much people that were come to the feast, when they heard that Jesus was coming to Jerusalem,
>
> 13 Took branches of palm trees, and went forth to meet him, and cried, Hosanna: Blessed is the King of Israel that cometh in the name of the Lord.
>
> John 12:12,13

Since being born again, I have seen some people come to church and start shouting, and they are still shouting after the benediction. I have seen some people dance for an hour straight and then fall out on the floor under what is called being slain in the Spirit. I have seen people who have interrupted the service by waiting for their particular moment to have a personal outbreak of what we call being overtaken in the Spirit.

Now, don't take me wrong. It is all right to praise God whenever and however you want, but I wonder, *how pure is our praise?*

In other words, how sincere is your shout? How deep is your devotion? How righteous is your running? How real is your dance? How serious is your jumping? How honest is your hallelujah? How true is your tongue speaking? How authentic is your adoration?

Are we just going through the motions, or is there something behind the noise that we make? We must be careful, because often we say words and don't realize what we have said. Words easily come out of our mouths, but most of them have to be followed up with action.

For instance, the words, "I love you." We say it when we get spring fever or when we get excited. We say it when somebody does something kind. We say it when a long overdue need has been met. We say it when we want something from somebody. We say it on Valentine's day. We say it when certain songs are played. But what about the action to follow?

Love is active and demonstrative. The scriptural definition of *love* in 1 Corinthians 13 is:

- It is patient.
- It is kind.
- It is not jealous.
- It does not boast.
- It is not arrogant.
- It doesn't act unseemly.
- It does not seek its own.
- It never fails.

How deep is your love? How sincere is your shout? How real is your righteousness? How pure is your praise?

My church has a reputation of being lively, on fire and noisy, but I wonder how much of it is real. I think a lot of our praise or noise-making is out of habit. We play, "Follow the leader." If the leader says, "Lift your hands and say, 'hallelujah,'" we say "hallelujah"! If the leader says, "Put your hands together and praise God," we put our hands together and lift Him up. If the leader says, "Turn to someone and say, 'I love you,'" we turn and tell someone we love them. If the leader says, "Stand up and give God some praise," we do so.

If our praise is pure, why can't we stand automatically? Why can't we spontaneously lift our hands? If our praise is pure, we won't need a leader to tell us when to say "hallelujah." The leader won't have to tell us when to clap our hands.

Not only is our praise sometimes habitual, at times it is hypocritical. You know, they've got so much spirit, it takes ten ushers to sit them down! They are so caught up in the Spirit, if you don't get out of their way, they'll knock you down and out! They've got so much Holy Ghost and so much praise, they are no earthly good to anyone!

Many of us wait until everyone finishes praising God and when everything is quiet and it's preaching time, we decide to holler. Or when it's time to go home, we decide to dance. The Bible speaks of a divine order. How pure is your praise?

When Jesus was making His triumphal entry into Jerusalem, it is recorded in each of the gospels that they took palm tree branches and went to meet Him. They hollered, "Hosanna, hallelujah, glory to the King!" But the same folks who hollered, *"Hosanna, hallelujah and glory to the King,"* hollered, "Crucify Him" on Friday!

That's what happens when your praise is hypocritical, when it is not real, when sincerity is missing, when it is habitual, when it comes only from the lips and not from the heart.

Yes, we make a lot of noise in our churches, but how much good noise are we making in our communities? in our homes? When we finish making noise, how many people have been saved? How many have been helped?

Yes, we shout and dance and jump, but when we come down, how straight do we walk? How holy do we live? We're shouting every Sunday, but we're still lying. We're dancing every Sunday and still committing adultery. We're speaking in tongues on Sunday, but we're still lying. We're running the walls every Sunday, but we're still getting high on drugs. We're falling out in the Spirit on Sunday, but we're still gossiping. We're clapping our hands on Sunday, but we're still raising hell. We're still shouting "Hosanna" on Sunday, but "Crucify Him" on Friday!

- How pure is your praise?
- How perfected is your peace?
- How sincere is your shout?
- How righteous is your running?
- How committed is your crying?
- How sweet is your singing?
- How authentic is your adoration?
- How deep is your devotion?
- How holy is your hallelujah?

The choir can sing all it wants to, but unless it is Spirit-anointed, it won't touch anyone. The preacher can preach until he turns blue in the face, climb every pew and turn somersaults in the aisles, but if it isn't Spirit-inspired, it won't reach anyone.

True praise is unushered. Pure praise is unrehearsed. Pure praise is unexpected.

When something you have been going through comes to a head, you can say "Hallelujah" all by yourself! When the Lord delivers you, you won't need any help. When you begin to think about where God has brought you from, your hands automatically go up and you won't need any help. This is pure praise.

When I think of the goodness of Jesus and all He has done for me, my soul cries out, "Hallelujah! Praise God for saving me!" This is pure praise.

When I think about the time I didn't have a dime, but the God I serve stepped in on time, I can say "Hallelujah" all by myself.

When I think about when I was sick and the doctors walked away and called my Mama and said, "We don't know what else to do," and in the middle of the night the preacher came and prayed the prayer of faith, look at me now. I can say "Hallelujah" all by myself.

When I think about when we lived in the project and sometimes we had hot water cornbread and syrup for dinner because we had no other choice, but now I eat it because I want to and I eat anything I want to, I can say "Hallelujah" all by myself.

When I think about when I was on my way to Finland, the plane took off from New York and a hurricane twirled the plane around in the air and God flew us on into Copenhagen, I can say "Hallelujah"!

When I think about when I was on my way to hell, too mean to live and not fit to die, He saved a wretch like me, I can say "Hallelujah"!

As Jesus went into the city, they took the palm branches and began to say, "Hosanna" and "Hallelujah," somebody said, "They are making too much noise." But Jesus said, "If they hold their peace, the rocks will surely cry out." As long as I live and have breath in my body, I don't want any rocks crying out for me!

In the next chapter, we will look at God's rain of abundance.

11
"I Smell Rain"

The Scripture passage from 1 Kings 18:41-46 speaks of "the sound of rain," while the passage from Job 14:7-9 speaks of "the scent of water." Both of these references are speaking of *God's blessings*.

Let's look at both of these Scripture references:

  41 And Elijah said unto Ahab, Get thee up, eat and drink; *for there is a sound of abundance of rain.*

  42 So Ahab went up to eat and to drink. And Elijah went up to the top of Carmel; and he cast himself down upon the earth, and put his face between his knees,

  43 And said to his servant, Go up now, look toward the sea. And he went up, and looked, and said, There is nothing. And he said, Go again seven times.

  44 And it came to pass at the seventh time, that he said, Behold, there ariseth a little cloud out of the sea, like a man's hand. And he said, Go up, say unto Ahab, Prepare thy chariot, and get thee down, that the rain stop thee not.

  45 And it came to pass in the mean while, that the heaven was black with clouds and wind, and there was a great rain. And Ahab rode, and went to Jezreel.

  46 And the hand of the Lord was on Elijah; and he girded up his loins, and ran before Ahab to the entrance of Jezreel.

          1 Kings 18:41-46

> 7 For there is hope of a tree, if it be cut down, that it will sprout again, and that the tender branch thereof will not cease.
>
> 8 Though the root thereof wax old in the earth, and the stock thereof die in the ground;
>
> 9 Yet through the *scent of water* it will bud, and bring forth boughs like a plant.
>
> **Job 14:7-9**

Do you need a blessing? Deliverance? Strength? I smell the rain! It's coming. It's about to happen. It's here!

It may seem a little unusual to you when I refer to rain as something we smell, but years ago, meteorology skills were lacking compared to today. Since it is very difficult to use the other four senses — taste, touch, sight and feel — when speaking of rain before it falls, God, in His infinite wisdom, sharpened the sense of smell so certain people would be able to tell others when rain is coming.

A marathon runner, when he has almost completed his run, in a state of exhaustion and completion, can smell and taste water before he gets to it.

A farmer, when he has experienced a period of drought and his crops are almost gone, after a time of prayer and escalating faith, smells rain coming.

A child of God who has been battered by the things of life, marching from "vision to victory," having spent time in the wilderness, time in labor and delivery, begins to prepare for a praise party because he smells the rain that is coming.

In Isaiah 43:20, God says, **I give waters in the wilderness, and rivers in the desert, to give drink to my people, my chosen.**

In the natural sense, rain is liquid precipitation that provides essential moisture for plants, animals and mankind.

The biblical writers believed that only the Lord, not the pagan gods, had control over the rain. This belief was strikingly confirmed several times in the Old Testament, especially through the predictions of Moses (Exodus 9:33,34); Samuel (1 Samuel 12:17,18); the prayers of Elijah (1 Kings 18:42-45); and God's announcement of the flood. (Genesis 7:4,10-12.)

In addition to these special occasions, God promised to send rain at the proper time (Leviticus 26:4; Deuteronomy 11:14), a promise which applied to all nations. (Matthew 5:45; Acts 14:17.)

Rain was a sign of God's blessing to the Israelites (Deuteronomy 28:12), although He could also hold back the rain, either as a warning (Amos 4:6,7), or as an expression of His judgment. (1 Kings 17:1; Jeremiah 3:3.)

In the Bible, *rain* is often a symbol of abundance. This abundance is compared with the effectiveness of God's Word (Deuteronomy 32:2; Isaiah 55:10), with the righteousness and peace of God's Kingdom (Psalm 72:6,7; Hosea 10:12), and with the wilderness. (Exodus 16:4; Psalm 78:24,27.)

Just as you can smell food cooking, the fragrance of cologne or perfume and the "new" smell of a vehicle just released from the manufacturer, you can reach a point in your spiritual pilgrimage where you can smell rain: The latter rain, the outpouring, the rain of cleansing, the rain of blessings, the rain of deliverance, the rain of completion and the rain of prosperity.

Even though you've been in a dry wilderness, I smell rain!

Even though you have been waiting for an answer to prayer, I smell rain!

Even though you have been seeking the fullness of God's Spirit, I smell rain!

Even though you need strength for your journey, I smell rain!

Even though you are sick of being sick, I smell rain!

If you are marching *from vision to victory*, I smell rain!

Get out your ponchos, your umbrella, your rain coat and scarf, for rain is coming to complete the work of the Lord!

Moving Out of Your Dry Season

To every thing there is a season.
Ecclesiastes 3:1

There is a reason for every season. I believe God allows dry seasons to keep us on track. A dry season doesn't mean you have done anything wrong. A good teacher doesn't always award his or her student with an "A," even though the student might deserve it. Sometimes, he or she gives the student a lesser grade so they will have something to work for and to keep them on their toes.

There are a variety of reasons as to why people hit dry seasons. Here are three of them:

1. *What is going on in your prayer life?*

Perhaps you used to pray regularly. You had a zeal to talk to the Lord and to spend time with Him, but you have allowed your schedule, fatigue, the children, the husband or wife and the job, or the boyfriend or girlfriend to stop you from doing what you know you ought to do.

What happened to the prayer line you used to be a part of? What happened to the "covenant" prayer partners you used to have? What happened to your early morning devotions? What happened to week-night prayer meetings? A bad prayer life is a "dry season."

James 5:13-18 says:

13 Is any among you afflicted? let him pray. Is any merry? let him sing psalms.

14 Is any sick among you? let him call for the elders of the church; and let them pray over him, anointing him with oil in the name of the Lord:

15 And the prayer of faith shall save the sick, and the Lord shall raise him up; and if he hath committed sins, they shall be forgiven him.

16 Confess your faults one to another, and pray one for another, that ye may be healed. The effectual fervent prayer of a righteous man availeth much.

17 Elias was a man subject to like passions as we are, and he prayed earnestly that it might not rain: and it rained not on the earth by the space of three years and six months.

18 And he prayed again, and the heaven gave rain, and the earth brought forth her fruit.

If there is little prayer, there will be little power. If there is much prayer, there will be much power. If there is no prayer, there will be no power.

Second Chronicles 7:13,14 says:

13 If I shut up heaven that there be no rain, or if I command the locusts to devour the land, or if I send pestilence among my people;

14 If my people, which are called by my name, shall humble themselves, and pray, and seek my face, and turn from their wicked ways; then will I hear from heaven, and will forgive their sin, and will heal their land.

2. *Are you inconsistent with God?*

Have you noticed that when some people are born again, they run diligently with the vision that is in their heart? Then down the road, they get sidetracked.

Absolutely nobody could stop you from going to church or supporting the ministry, but now there is a "serious gap" and you have become inconsistent.

You used to go to church every Sunday. Now you go every now and then. You used to go to Bible study. Now you go seasonally. You used to be involved in ministry. Now you are a part of the bench society. God is not pleased, and your inconsistency is causing you to experience a dry season.

Your wood is wet. Your wick is out. Your wax is cold. Your joy is limited. Your thrill is gone. Your transmission has sprung a leak. Your engine has thrown a rod. Your clapper doesn't ring anymore. You are experiencing a dry season.

3. *Who are you hanging around with?*

Are the people you fellowship with negative, unspiritual, fighting, doubting God's ability, emphasizing what you can't do? If you will change your attitude as well as your acquaintances, watch your dry season change!

If you are going to make it from vision to victory, hang around people who are strong in the Lord.

Look Again for the Rain!

If you haven't seen the manifestation of God's rain of blessings and abundance in your life, look again for the sound of rain just as Elijah did.

The Prophet Elijah told Ahab that it was going to rain. After prayer, the prophet told his servants to go and look toward the sea. They did, but they saw nothing. However, when they came back to the man of God, he said, **Go again seven times** (1 Kings 18:43). Then they began to see the formation of the storm clouds.

This is so crucial in the walk of faith. Many times things will not look like they are going to happen, but we must have faith enough to go look again.

When you look at a church for the first time, it may look like a people in flux, a ball of confusion, or a bunch of hypocrites, but put on your spiritual eyeglasses and look again. You will begin to see God's vision unfolding before your eyes.

When you first look at your finances, you may see that you don't have enough to make it through the end of the week. But when faith comes in, look again and you will see that you will make it.

When you first look at the terminal illness in your body,

look again and you will see, "By His stripes I am healed." When you first look and see the burdens of this world, look again and you will see, there is a great day coming! Faith doesn't look at what is. It looks again to what God has spoken.

Hebrews 11:1 says, **Now faith is the substance of things hoped for, the evidence of things not seen.**

Faith says...

- I can conquer all circumstances.
- I can destroy all doubts.
- I can defeat all discouragement.
- I can overcome all opposition.
- I can face all fears.
- I can defy all devils.

Have enough faith to look again and you will be confident that you can...

- Fight all battles.
- Resist all temptations.
- Endure all trials.
- Survive all tests.
- Bear all burdens.

Faith says, "I can minister as the Holy Spirit directs." Faith says, "I can fulfill all of my commitments."

The first time I looked at the task in front of me, I said, "It is too much for me to do." The first time I looked at the building our church is now housed in, I said to the trustees, "It's too much for us to afford." The first time I looked at the house where I now live, I said, "My credit will never be approved." The first time I thought about adding another service, I said, "The people will never come."

Thank God, I had faith to look again and realize that with the Holy Spirit's empowerment and guidance, I could...

- Fulfill my commitments.
- Drive what I want to drive.
- Live where I want to live.
- Build what I want to build.
- Go where I want to go.
- Have what I want to have.

If you will look again, you will...

- Reach the unreachable.
- Endure the unendurable.
- Love the unlovable.
- Forgive the unforgivable.
- Bear the unbearable.
- Face the unfaceable.

I smell the abundance of rain! God's abundance is on its way to you right now, in Jesus' precious and holy name. Amen.

Expect More Than a "Sprinkle"

It's time to take God out of your little box. We serve a God Who is *well able* **to do exceeding abundantly above all that we ask or think, according to the power that worketh in us** (Ephesians 3:20).

After Elijah prayed for rain, Scripture says, **There was a *great* rain** (1 Kings 18:45).

God does more than sprinkle! I not only smell rain, but I smell a great rain!

You may be one who could have died from spiritual dehydration, but I smell the rain! It is possible that you could have died in the wilderness of life, but I smell the rain! You could have passed out, been written off, been excluded from the will and counted as a nothing. But go ahead and dig some deep ditches, because God's showers of blessings are coming and they will fill the ditches!

Paul said:

> 8 We are troubled on every side, yet not distressed; we are perplexed, but not in despair;
>
> 9 Persecuted, but not forsaken; cast down, but not destroyed;
>
> 10 Always bearing about in the body the dying of the Lord Jesus, that the life also of Jesus might be made manifest in our body.
>
> **2 Corinthians 4:8-10**

I smell the abundance of rain coming to you, your spouse, your family, your church and all of your relationships! God's blessings are about to overtake you!

In the final chapter, I want to encourage you to go on out into the deep, because that's where God will meet you and team up with you so you can do great exploits for Him!

12
Go On Out Into the Deep!

11 Mine eye also shall see my desire on mine enemies, and mine ears shall hear my desire of the wicked that rise up against me.

12 The righteous shall flourish like the palm tree: he shall grow like a cedar in Lebanon.

13 *Those that be planted in the house of the Lord shall flourish in the courts of our God.*

14 They shall still bring forth fruit in old age; they shall be fat and flourishing;

15 To shew that the Lord is upright: he is my rock, and there is no unrighteousness in him.

Psalm 92:11-15

This is an exciting time in which to live, and God wants us to live it abundantly.

The days of prideful, unholy men preaching cheap grace and misrepresenting the character of God are over! The days of having a little bit of Jesus and a touch of the Holy Ghost are over! The days for having just a plain, ordinary Christian experience but no personal relationship are over!

There is a place of identification with Christ where we take on His character and fragrance. It's called *the age of the anointing*. This is the age of the outpouring that Joel spoke of:

28 And it shall come to pass afterward, that I will pour out my spirit upon all flesh; and your sons

> and your daughters shall prophesy, your old men shall dream dreams, your young men shall see visions:
>
> 29 And also upon the servants and upon the handmaids in those days will I pour out my spirit.
>
> Joel 2:28,29

This is the age of the moving of God's Spirit. This is the age when called, chosen and faithful servants are learning the price of testing and God is anointing them with fresh fire and oil.

The anointing, simply stated, is the *pneuma* of God — the breath of God — or better yet, the power and presence of the Holy Spirit on an individual's life and ministry.

When I was growing up, I thought it was just enough to go to church. I mean, anybody who went to church regularly was already considered different. So I thought all you had to do was obey your parents, get good grades in school and go to church. That's not enough! There is a higher height and a deeper depth in Christ Jesus.

It is your choice to have just a regular Christian experience or to have the peace, love, joy and anointing of the Holy Spirit. The anointing is costly. In other words, you will go through something to reach higher heights in God. Whatever you are going through today for the cause of Christ may be the price you are paying for a new anointing.

In the production of a movie, there is one person who is never seen, but without him, no movie would ever become a finished product. He's called the "director." In the realm of the Spirit, the Holy Spirit is the One Who works behind the scenes in our behalf. John 16:8-12 says He teaches and He convicts. Romans 8 says He guides, assures, prays and intercedes for us. But throughout the Bible, one of His crucial ministries is that of *anointing*.

Why is God preparing us for a new anointing?

- There are new demonic tricks and traps.
- There are new occult movements.

- There are new adversities.
- There are new cults.
- There are drugs in every community.
- There are suicides in every race.
- There are white-collar criminals across the land.
- There is a rapid spread of immorality in this country and around the world.
- There is an absence of the fear of the Lord throughout the world.
- Our government is in trouble.
- Our schools are in trouble.
- Our youth are in trouble.
- Our streets are in trouble.
- Our churches are in trouble.

Consequently, we must be equipped to deal with hurting people and stand on the front lines and present a ray of hope that is found only in Christ Jesus!

God is ready to bring about an outpouring of His Spirit for those of us who will receive it. God will never leave His saints without the proper equipment to deal with the enemy.

Malachi 3:3-6 says:

3 And he shall sit as a refiner and purifier of silver: and he shall purify the sons of Levi, and purge them as gold and silver, that they may offer unto the Lord an offering in righteousness.

4 Then shall the offering of Judah and Jerusalem be pleasant unto the Lord, as in the days of old, and as in former years.

5 And I will come near to you to judgment; and I will be a swift witness against the sorcerers, and against the adulterers, and against false swearers, and against those that oppress the hireling in his

wages, the widow, and the fatherless, and that turn aside the stranger from his right, and fear not me, saith the Lord of hosts.

6   For I am the Lord, I change not; therefore ye sons of Jacob are not consumed.

If you want a new anointing, you must look up!

Romans 12:2 in the *J. B. Phillips Translation* says, **Don't let the world around you squeeze you into its own mold, but let God re-make you so that your whole attitude of mind is changed.**

The anointing makes you look up when the things of the world would have you look down. The anointing will give you new vision. We need God's vision to establish goals and fulfill our destiny in His Kingdom.

Without the anointing of the Holy Spirit, we will never act on earth like we will act in heaven. Those who live without a vision and without a purpose will live in hopelessness and depression. Proverbs 29:18 says, **Where there is no vision, the people perish.** Look up!

The anointing opens up your ears so you can hear God's voice. As sons and daughters of God, we must be led by the Spirit of God. Look up!

People who have been in church a long time seem to become stiff, starchy and legalistic. Yet God wants us to grow in the knowledge of His grace, not the works of the law. Look up!

Then He says the righteous shall flourish like the palm tree and shall grow like cedars in Lebanon. The palm tree has deep roots and searches out the waters in desert places. The cedars have long life and grow very tall. In other words, the anointing will aid us in finding watering places in deserts and during dry seasons. If we observe God's principles and receive His anointing, we will have a rich, long life and we will grow tall. Look up!

If you want a new anointing, you must look within.

Your heart must be right. Your attitude must be right. Your desire must be holiness.

Spend more time looking within yourself rather than someone else. David searched himself. In Psalm 51:10-12 he said:

> **10 Create in me a clean heart, O God; and renew a right spirit within me.**
>
> **11 Cast me not away from thy presence; and take not thy holy spirit from me.**
>
> **12 Restore unto me the joy of thy salvation; and uphold me with thy free spirit.**

There must be a softening of your heart. You cannot have the anointing and still have a haughty spirit or a bad attitude.

> **36 And he spake also a parable unto them; No man putteth a piece of a new garment upon an old; if otherwise, then both the new maketh a rent, and the piece that was taken out of the new agreeth not with the old.**
>
> **37 And no man putteth new wine into old bottles; else the new wine will burst the bottles, and be spilled, and the bottles shall perish.**
>
> **38 But new wine must be put into new bottles; and both are preserved.**
>
> **39 No man also having drunk old wine straightway desireth new: for he saith, The old is better.**
>
> **Luke 5:36-39**

The old, crusty wineskins were first dipped in water to restore the moisture. This is symbolic of our heart being moistened and softened by the washing of the water of God's Word.

Without cleansing we build up walls of resistance and unbelief which keep us hostage from moving where God would have us go. Look within!

The wineskins were then rubbed with fresh oil, which is representative of a new anointing in our lives. This is the ability to move on and walk in the new wine of His Spirit. Look within!

In order to receive the anointing of the Holy Spirit, you must be obedient in a local assembly. I'm talking about being involved in church and sitting under the teaching of the Word, allowing God to deal with you in the areas that would hinder your life. Everyone who wants a new anointing must be in a local church under an anointed man or woman of God. Everyone who wants the anointing must be in a regular Bible study or Sunday school so the inner man can be fed spiritually.

Psalm 92 says if you want to flourish in the courts of God, you must be planted in the house, meaning the local church. God has a divine plan with divine order.

If a baseball player hits a home run, I don't care how far he hits the ball, I don't care how much the crowds are excited, I don't care how much the reporter covers the story, he is in danger of being called "out" if he doesn't touch home plate.

You must make sure that within everything in your power, you are all right with first base if you want the anointing to be present in what you are doing.

If you want a new anointing, you must look ahead in faith.

The pressures that we experience in this life often make us think we are not going to make it very far. The temptations we deal with often make us think that we are not going to be able to report victory. The sorrows of life will attempt to keep you sad, but when the anointing comes, things change!

When the anointing comes, you will be able to look ahead. When the anointing is present, no matter what the devil throws at you, you can look him in the eye and say, "Next." No matter how the winds of this life beat on you, you can look at them and say, "Next."

When the anointing comes, though trouble may be present, you can look Satan eye to eye and stand toe to toe with him and say, "It's hallelujah anyhow"!

You can count on making it. You can count on being in the mix. You can count on being strong. You can count on being victorious because of the anointing.

Isaiah 43:18,19 says:

18 Remember ye not the former things, neither consider the things of old.

19 Behold, I will do a new thing; now it shall spring forth; shall ye not know it? I will even make a way in the wilderness, and rivers in the desert.

The new anointing will allow you to look ahead.

• Expect God to save your family because of His promise in Acts 16:31 and because of the new anointing.

• Expect God to do something about your finances, because of the promises of His Word and because of the new anointing.

• Expect God to give you a new house.

• Expect God to give you a promotion.

• Expect your deliverance...all because of the new anointing.

Some folks take cigarette breaks. Others take rest breaks. And yet others take mental breaks. I dare you to stop what you are doing and take a praise break!

When we take a praise break, we tell God "thank You," and He says, "You are welcome." While we are in the break, our minds are not on anything else but praising God.

Praise breaks make depression leave. It makes demons behave. It will bring good news to the poor, according to Isaiah. It will bring deliverance to the captives and set them free.

Praise breaks can be compared to putting on new clothes. You can put them on or take them off. But if you wear the new all the time, it will...

- Ward off spirits of evil.
- Ward off spirits of depression.
- Ward off spirits of discouragement.
- Ward off spirits of despair.

Remember, the anointing gives us faith to look ahead. God will make a way for you in the wilderness, and He will make rivers in your desert. He will make the crooked places straight and the rough places smooth.

When the anointing comes, your ability is exchanged for God's ability. When it comes, whatever He is, you become. If He is righteous, you become righteous. If He is holy, you become holy. If He is strong, you become strong. If He is victorious, you become victorious. If He is loving, you become loving. If He is joy, you become joy.

It's a new day.

It's a new way.

It's a new thing.

It's a new swing.

It's a new ploy.

It's a new joy!

And this joy that we now have, the world didn't give it to us, and neither can the world take it away!

As you go out into the deep spiritually, there are some important things that you need to be mindful of.

After over fifty years of preaching and fourteen years of pastoring, I have had the privilege of visiting and ministering in many churches throughout the world. My saddest discovery is that of finding so many ministries without the liberty to praise. Many churches and believers are living beneath their privileges. Praise is required of us, and it is beneficial to us.

Here are some steps to changing from a traditional, regimented church service to a free and flowing praise atmosphere:

1. The pastor/leader must be Spirit filled and Spirit led. (John 4:24.)

2. The pastor/leader must be an example in praise. (Psalm 34:1-3.)

3. The people must be taught that praise is a way of life rather than a Sunday event. (Ephesians 5:18-20.)

4. There must be an openness of the people to move from tradition to Spirit-led worship.

5. There must be regular preaching and teaching on the subject of praise.

6. There must be a removal of all limitations and boundaries that have been set on spiritual beliefs. (1 Thessalonians 5:19-24.)

7. The fear of stepping over the line to obey the command of God to praise must be removed. (Psalm 150:1-6.)

I believe God has implanted certain people in the Body of Christ who must serve as catalysts to liberate people in this area. It has become part of my mandate to saturate the lives of all those I touch with a new look at praise.

Many people and churches are dying because of the mere fact that they have not been introduced to this vehicle and ordinance that God has given to us. Praise is not just for the musically inclined; it is for every child of God. I encourage you to go out into the deep and unlock the blessing of praise.

Many feats are incomplete, inaccurate and/or impossible without a life of praise. You will not have a strong anointing upon your life if you are not a praiser. You will be limited in your operation in the Spirit if you are not a praiser.

You will be hindered in your ministry efforts if you are not a praiser. Praise is perhaps the most hidden secret of the successful Christian's life.

In this book, we have discussed many critical principles as they relate to praise. Prayerfully apply them to your life, take authority over your situations and move to a higher level in God. Then your vision will, without any doubt, be turned into victory!

Now, I command you to go forth and give God the high praise. I am excited about your future!